Made in the USA
Middletown, DE
03 October 2024

61973081R00057